Christmas 1970

A starter for your book collection.

<u>A Family</u> Prayer

When the golden sun is
          setting
And from care your mind
          is free
And of absent ones you're
          thinking,
Will you sometimes think
          of me?

          All my love
                    Mimi

TREASURED VOLUME

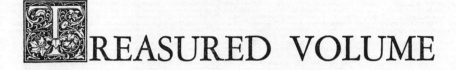

TREASURED VOLUME

An Anthology of Poems

COLLECTED BY JOHN SCOTT

An Oak Tree Press Book
PUBLISHED BY
THE C. R. GIBSON COMPANY
NORWALK, CONNECTICUT

for Toretta

. . . but first, a word

THERE is a kind of poetry ignored by the schools and critics which lives on in the hearts of men, the kind of song which Longfellow recognized in "The Day is Done," when he noted the need for "some simple and heartfelt lay"—one "from the treasured volume."

This *Treasured Volume* is a collection of such poems, put together at random, for the reader who is looking for the shared experience which always means so much to all of us, the word of consolation or assurance which each of us needs too often, the new look at old woes which makes them lighter—even the smile we can all enjoy.

Although presented at random—changing in mood as the pages turn, just as our own moods change with the turning pages of our calendar—none of these poems found its way into the *Treasured Volume* by accident. Many were chosen as the result of wide, deep interest expressed by my radio audience after they had been read over WOR on my program, "Radio New York." When the mail brought thousands of requests for copies and there was no anthology in which they were collected, it was obvious that this book was needed.

The only possible explanation for such a response is that the poems are, as Longfellow put it, songs that gushed from the heart. And there was startling confirmation of his words when it turned out that almost all the selections came—to use his words—"from some humbler poet." Indeed, in many cases, though the words and thought of a poem have lived on, the poet himself has been forgotten—dropped into the anonymity of "Anonymous"—and his name cannot be recovered. That's why a number of poems in *Treasured Volume* carry no name at the end. The author is unknown.

But whether the author is known or not, his lines—if they are here—have stood the test of time, even though he's not one of Longfellow's "bards sublime." Some of these bards, it is true, have found a page in the *Treasured Volume,* but it is interesting to note that it is the lesser works of such men which have met the test: a sonnet from Milton—not his epic; a bit from Shakespeare's *Merchant of Venice*—not from his masterwork, *Hamlet.*

But I think that's enough. The purpose of *Treasured Volume* is to bring you the poems which follow.

JOHN SCOTT

[8]

CONTENTS

[11]

❧ TREASURED VOLUME ❧

HE DAY is done, and the darkness
    Falls from the wings of night,
As a feather is wafted downward
    From an eagle in his flight.

I see the lights of the village
    Gleam through the rain and the mist,
And a feeling of sadness comes o'er me
    That my soul cannot resist:

A feeling of sadness and longing,
    That is not akin to pain,
And resembles sorrow only
    As the mist resembles the rain.

Come, read to me some poem—
    Some simple and heartfelt lay
That shall soothe this restless feeling,
    And banish the cares of day.

Not from the grand old masters,
    Not from the bards sublime,
Whose distant footsteps echo
    Through the corridors of Time.

For, like strains of martial music,
    Their mighty thoughts suggest

Life's endless toil and endeavor,
    And tonight I long for rest.

Read from some humbler poet
    Whose songs gushed from his heart,
As showers from the clouds of summer,
    Or tears from the eyelids, start;

Who, through long days of labor,
    And nights devoid of ease,
Still heard in his soul the music
    Of wonderful melodies.

Such songs have power to quiet
    The restless pulse of care,
And come like the benediction
    That follows after prayer.

Then read from the treasured volume
    The poem of your choice,
And lend to the rhyme of the poet
    The beauty of your voice.

And the night shall be filled with music
    And the cares, that infest the day,
Shall fold their tents, like the Arabs,
    And as silently steal away.

Henry Wadsworth Longfellow

[16]

GIVE THEM THE FLOWERS NOW

LOSED eyes can't see the white roses,
 Cold hands can't hold them, you know,
 Breath that is stilled cannot gather
 The odors that sweet from them blow.
Death, with a peace beyond dreaming,
 The children of earth does endow;
Life is the time we can help them,
 So give them the flowers now!

Here are the struggles and striving,
 Here are the cares and the tears;
Now is the time to be smoothing
 Life's frowns and the troubles and fears;
What to closed eyes are kind sayings?
 What to hushed heart is deep vow?
Naught can avail after parting,
 So give them the flowers now!

Just a kind word or a greeting;
 Just a warm grasp or a smile—
These are the flowers that will lighten
 The burdens for many a mile.
After the journey is over
 What is the use of them; how
Can they carry them who are carried?
 Oh, give them the flowers now!

Blooms from the happy heart's garden
　　Plucked in the spirit of love;
Blooms that are earthly reflections
　　Of flowers that blossom above.
Words cannot tell what a measure
　　Of blessings such gifts will allow
To dwell in the lives of many,
　　So give them the flowers now!

Leigh M. Hodges

❧ HOW TO PRAY ❧

HE PROPER WAY for a man to pray,"
　　Said Deacon Lemuel Keyes,
"And the only proper attitude
　　Is down upon his knees."

"No, I should say the way to pray,"
　　Said Reverend Doctor Wise,
"Is standing straight with outstretched arms
　　And rapt and upturned eyes."

"Oh, no; no, no," said Elder Slow,
　　"Such posture is too proud;
A man should pray with eyes fast closed
　　And head contritely bowed."

“It seems to me his hands should be
  Austerely clasped in front,
With both thumbs pointing toward the ground,”
  Said Reverend Doctor Blunt.

“Last year I fell in Hodgkins’ well
  Head first,” said Cyrus Brown,
“With both my heels a-sticking up,
  My head a-pointing down;

“And I made a prayer right then and there—
  Best prayer I ever said,
The prayingest prayer I ever prayed,
  A-standing on my head.”

Sam Walter Foss

DAWN

Day’s sweetest moments are at dawn.
Refreshed by his long sleep, the Light
Kisses the languid lips of Night
Ere she can rise and hurry on;
All glowing from his dreamless rest
He holds her closely to his breast—
Warm lip to lip and limb to limb—
Until she dies for love of him.

Ella Wheeler Wilcox

F YOU'VE anything good to say of a man,
 Don't wait till he's laid to rest,
 For the eulogy spoken when hearts are broken
  Is an empty thing at best.
Ah! the blighted flower now drooping lonely
 Would perfume the mountain-side,
If the sun's glad ray had but shone one day
 Before, in the bud, it died.

If you've any alms to give to the poor,
 Don't wait till you hear the cry
Of wan distress in the wilderness,
 Lest the one forsaken die.
Oh, harken to poverty's sad lament!
 Be swift her wants to allay;
Don't spurn God's poor from the favored door,
 As you hope for mercy one day.

Don't wait for another to share the burden
 Of sorrow's most mournful load;
Let your hand now extend to the stricken friend
 Who is stumbling down life's road;
And if you've anything good to say of a man,
 Don't wait till he's laid to rest;
For the eulogy spoken when hearts are broken
 Is an empty thing at best.

ONG, long before the Babe could speak,
When He would kiss His mother's cheek
And to her bosom press,
The brightest angels standing near
Would turn away to hide a tear—
For they are motherless.

John B. Tabb

❧ BEAUTIFUL HANDS ❧

UCH beautiful, beautiful hands,
They're neither white nor small;
And you, I know, would scarcely think
That they were fair at all.
I've looked on hands whose form and hue
A sculptor's dream might be,
Yet are those aged wrinkled hands
Most beautiful to me.

[21]

Such beautiful, beautiful hands!
  Though heart were weary and sad,
Those patient hands kept toiling on
  That the children might be glad.
I almost weep when looking back
  To childhood's distant day!
I think how those hands rested not
  When mine were at their play.

Such beautiful, beautiful hands!
  They're growing feeble now,
For time and pain have left their mark
  On hand, and heart and brow.
Alas! Alas! the nearing time—
  The sad, sad day to me—
When life is gone and out of sight,
  Those hands will folded be.

But on beyond these passing lands,
  Where all is bright and fair,
I know full well those dear old hands
  Will palms of victory bear;
Where crystal streams through endless years
  Flow over golden sands,
And where the old are young again,
  I'll clasp my mother's hands.

Ellen M. H. Gates

VERY DAY is a fresh new beginning,
    Every morning the world's made new;
    You who are weary of sorrow and sinning:
      Here is a beautiful hope for you—
A hope for me and a hope for you.

All the past things are all gone and over,
    Tasks are complete and the tears are shed;
Yesterday's errors let yesterday cover;
    Yesterday's wounds, which once smarted and bled,
    Are healed with the healing which night has shed.

Yesterday now is a part of forever,
    Bound in a sheaf, which our God holds tight:
Glad days and sad days and bad days which never
    Come back to us with their bloom or blight—
    Their fullness of sunshine or sorrowful night.

So let them go, since we cannot relive them,
    Cannot undo what we once have done;
Only God's mercy, we know, can forgive them;
    Ours is the new day, and ours alone
    When for past errors we can atone.

Here are the skies newly blue, burnished brightly,
  Here is the spent Earth now all reborn,
Here are the weary limbs now rested and lightly
  Springing to meet the new day's new morn,
  In the chrism of dew and the cool of the dawn.

Every day is a fresh new beginning;
  Listen, my soul, to the glad refrain,
Cast off old sorrow and older sinning,
  Problems forecast, even possible pain,
  Take heart with the day: begin new again.

Susan Coolidge

☙ THE TAPER ❧

NE TAPER lights a thousand,
  Yet shines as it has shone;
And the humblest light may kindle
  A brighter than its own.

Hezekiah Butterworth

OWN the lane, and across the fields,
    Doris and I were walking.
Past bulging stacks that the harvest yields,
    Doris and I were talking.

"The man I wed," said Doris fair,
   (Doris did most of the talking)
"Must be a multi-millionaire."
   I only kept on walking.

"His hair must be yellow, his eyes dark blue,"
   ('Twas Doris doing the talking)
"And he must be a Yale man, too.
   "Isn't it lovely, walking?"

Now I am poor, and my hair is brown,
   (I never was much at talking)
And I came from Harvard, in Cambridge town
   (I'm really quite good at walking).

But I slipped my arm 'round Doris sweet
   (She suddenly stopped her talking)
And I hugged her nearly off her feet—
   'Twas really a help to walking.

[25]

And I said, "I'm sorry I don't suit you."
    (Somehow we'd stopped our walking.)
But, "Oh," said Doris, "I guess you'll do."
    For Doris was only talking.

Clarence S. Harper

❧ SERVICE ☙

O DUTY, the best of lives are wed
By action, noble and small
The tight knit bonds of service
Love, enriching all.

Fame may never find you
In stories for others to read
But The Book of Life is witness
To every blessed deed

Your love will sing its own blessing
To bring you happiness
A poor man helped and ill man served
It is in action we are blessed.

HAT would we do in this world of ours,
    Were it not for the dreams ahead?
For thorns are mixed with the blooming flowers,
    No matter which path we tread.

And each of us has his golden goal,
    Stretching far into the years;
And ever he climbs with a hopeful soul,
    With alternate smiles and tears.

That dream ahead is what holds man up
    Through the storms of a ceaseless fight;
When his lips are pressed to the wormwood's cup,
    And clouds shut out the light.

To some it's a dream of high estate;
    To some it's a dream of wealth;
To some it's a dream of a truce with Fate
    In a constant search for health.

To some it's a dream of home and wife;
    To some it's a crown above;
The dreams ahead are what make each life:
    The dreams—and faith—and love!

Edwin Carlile Litsey

ON A BRIDGE I was standing one morning
And watching the current roll by,
When suddenly into the water
There fell an unfortunate fly.

The fishes that swam to the surface
Were looking for something to eat,
And I thought that the helpless young insect
Would surely afford them a treat.

"Poor thing!" I exclaimed with compassion,
"Your trials and dangers abound,
For if you escape being eaten,
You cannot escape being drowned."

No sooner the sentence was spoken
Than lo, like an angel of love,
I saw, to the waters beneath me,
A little leaf fall from above.

It glided serene on the water,
Like an ark for the poor little fly;
Which soon to the land reascending,
Spread its wings in the breezes to dry.

O sweet was the truth that was whispered,
   That mortals should never despair,
For He who takes care of an insect,
   Much more for His children will care.

And though to our short-sighted vision,
   No way of escape may appear;
Let us trust; for when least we expect it,
   The help of Our Father is near.

Adapted from an old book of Welsh songs and poems

✍ MOTHER ଛ

THE NOBLEST thoughts my soul can claim,
The holiest words my tongue can frame,
Unworthy are to praise the name
   More sacred than all other.

An infant, when her love first came—
Now man, I find it just the same;
Reverently I breathe her name:
   The blessed name of mother.

George Griffith Fetter

ID YOU tackle the trouble that came your way
    With a resolute heart and cheerful?
Or hide your face from the light of day
    With a craven soul and fearful?
Oh, a trouble's a ton, or a trouble's an ounce,
    Or a trouble is what you make it,
And it isn't the fact that you're hurt that counts,
    But only how did you take it?

You are beaten to earth? Well, well!
    Come up with a smiling face.
It's nothing against you to fall down flat,
    But to lie there—that's disgrace.
The harder you're thrown, why, the higher you bounce;
    Be proud of your blackened eye!
It isn't the fact that you're licked that counts;
    It's how did you fight—and why?

And though you be done to the death, what then?
    If you battled the best you could,
If you played your part in the world of men,
    Rest in peace; they will call you good.
Death comes with a crawl, or comes with a pounce,
    And whether he's slow or spry,
It isn't the fact that you're dead that counts,
    But only—how did you die?

Edmund Vance Cooke

SING the song of the workman,
 The joy of the man whose hand
 Leaps to fulfill with practised skill
  The keen, sure brain's demand,
Who knows the thrill of creation,
 Who stands with the Lord as one—
Sees what was wrought from hidden thought
 And can say of his work, "Well done!"

Others may seek for rank and wealth,
 And search the wide world through—
He knows the deep where grand thoughts sleep,
 Which Tubal-cain once knew.
Beauty may lie in a woman's eye,
 And dwell on her lips so sweet—
It lies as well in the engine's swell,
 And the piston's throbbing beat.

The arch which defies the river's flood,
 And holds its waves in check,
Is fair as the line where tresses twine,
 Or the curve of a snowy neck;
And he who can feel such beauty's power,
 And bid it live and move,
Knows a deeper bliss than a maiden's kiss
 Can give to the heart of love.

He gladly greets the coming years—
    They bring him added skill;
He feels no ruth for the loss of youth—
    His goal is nearer still.
And only this he asks of fate:
    That he may keep his dower
Of strength, and will, and labor's skill,
    Until his life's last hour.

Ninette M. Lowater

CUPIDO

HE SOLID, solid universe
    Is pervious to Love;
With bandaged eyes he never errs,
    Around, below, above.
His blinding light
He flingeth white
On God's and Satan's brood,
And reconciles
By mystic wiles
The evil and the good.

Ralph Waldo Emerson

THE MAID who binds her warrior's sash
    With smile that well her pain dissembles,
    The while beneath her drooping lash
      One starry teardrop hangs and trembles,
Though Heaven alone records the tear,
    And fame shall never know her story,
Her heart has shed a drop as dear
    As ever fell on field of glory!

The wife who girds her husband's sword
    'Mid little ones who weep or wonder
And bravely speaks the cheering word,
    Although her heart be rent asunder,
Doomed nightly in her dreams to hear
    The bolts of death around him rattle,
Has shed as sacred blood as e'er
    Was poured upon the field of battle!

The mother who conceals her grief
    While to her breast her son she presses,
Then says a few words brave and brief,
    Kissing the patriot brow she blesses,
With no one but her secret God
    To know the pain that weighs upon her,
Sheds holy blood as ever sod
    Received on freedom's field of honor!

Thomas Buchanan Read

[33]

THE NIGHT has a thousand eyes,
  And the day but one,
    Yet the light of the bright world dies
      With the dying sun.

The mind has a thousand eyes,
  And the heart but one,
And the light of a whole life dies
  When its love is done.

Francis W. Bourdillon

❧ THE CREATION ❧

LL THINGS bright and beautiful,
  All creatures, great and small,
    All things wise and wonderful—
      The Lord God made them all:

Each little flower that opens,
  Each little bird that sings—
He made their glowing colors,
  He made their tiny wings:

The purple-headed mountain,
    The river running by,
The sunset and the morning
    That brightens up the sky:

The cold wind in the winter,
    The pleasant summer sun,
The ripe fruits in the garden—
    He made them every one:

The tall trees in the forest,
    The meadows filled with hay,
The rushes by the water
    We gather every day—

He gave us eyes to see them,
    And lips that we might tell
How great is God Almighty,
    Who has made all things well!

Cecil Frances Alexander

❧ A FAMILY PRAYER ☙

WHEN the golden sun is setting
And from care your mind is free,
And of absent ones you're thinking,
Will you sometimes think of me?

THE THING that goes the furthest toward making life
    worth while,
    That costs the least and does the most, is just a
    pleasant smile.
The smile that bubbles from a heart that loves its fellow-men
Will drive away the cloud of gloom and coax the sun again;
It's full of worth and better, too, with much of kindness blent:
It's worth a million dollars, and it doesn't cost a cent.

There is no room for sadness when we see a cheery smile;
It always has the same good look—it's never out of style;
It nerves us on to try again when failure makes us blue;
The dimples of encouragement are good for me and you.
It pays good interest through the years, for it is merely lent—
It's worth a million dollars, and it doesn't cost a cent.

A smile comes very easy—you can wrinkle up with cheer
A hundred times before you can squeeze out a soggy tear;
It ripples out, moreover; other hearts will feel the tug,
And smiles will soon surround you in a crushing, bear-like hug.
So, smile away, folks; understand what by a smile is meant.
It's worth a million dollars, and it doesn't cost a cent.

W. D. Nesbit

HICH shall it be? Which shall it be?
I looked at John; John looked at me;
And when I found that I must speak,
My voice seemed strangely low and weak:
And then I listened while he read.
"This is his letter: '*I will give*
A house and land while you shall live,
If in return to me is given
One child of yours. Just one. You've seven.'"

I looked at John's old clothes, so worn
By all the work that he had borne;
I thought of seven young mouths to feed—
Of seven little children's needs.
And then of this. "Come, John," said I,
"We'll choose among them as they lie
Asleep." So walking hand in hand
Dear John and I surveyed our band:
First to the cradle softly stepped
Where Lilian, the baby, slept.
Gently her father stopped to lay
His rough hand down in a loving way
To stop the dream that made her stir
And huskily he said, "Not her."

We stooped beside the trundle bed
And one long ray of lamplight shed
Upon the two boys' faces there—
The twins, so beautiful and fair.
Here was—perhaps—a duplicate;
But who had heart to separate
These two so much like one another
That each to each was more than brother?

Pale patient Robbie's angel face
Still in his sleep bore suffering's trace.
"No—not for a thousand crowns—not him,"
John whispered. And our eyes were dim.

Poor Dick, bad Dick? Our wayward son—
Turbulent, restless, idle one—
Could he be spared? No, He who gave
Bade us befriend Dick to the grave;
Only a mother's heart could be
Patient enough for such as he.
"Oh, no," said John, "I would not dare
To take him from your daily prayer."

Then to the stairs, and up above
We knelt by Mary, child of love.
"Perhaps for her 't would better be,"
I said to John. Quite silently
He lifted up a curl that lay
Across her cheek in a willful way.
My heart stood still in dreadful fear.
John shook his head: "We'll keep her here."

Only one more, our eldest lad:
Trusty and truthful, good and glad—
So like his father. "No, John, no;
I cannot, will not let him go."

And so we wrote, in a courteous way,
We could not give one child away.
And afterward, toil lighter seemed,
Thinking of that of which we dreamed,
Happy in truth that not one face
Was missed from its accustomed place;
Thankful to work for all the seven;
Trusting the rest to One in Heaven.

Ethel Lynn-Beers

⤙ WHOLE DUTY OF CHILDREN ⤚

 CHILD should always say what's true
And speak when he is spoken to,
And eat with manners at the table
—At least as far as he is able.

Robert Louis Stevenson

[39]

TASTE a liquor never brewed,
   From tankards scooped in pearl;
Not all the vats upon the Rhine
   Yield such an alcohol!

Inebriate of air am I,
   And debauchee of dew,
Reeling, through endless summer days,
   From inns of molten blue.

When landlords turn the drunken bee
   Out of the foxglove's door,
When butterflies renounce their drams,
   I shall but drink the more!

Till seraphs swing their snowy hats,
   And saints to windows run,
To see the little tippler
   Leaning against the sun!

Emily Dickinson

OCK OF AGES, cleft for me,
Let me hide myself in Thee;
Let the water and the blood,
From Thy wounded side which flowed,
Be of sin the double cure.
Save from wrath and make me pure.

Could my tears forever flow,
Could my zeal no languor know,
These for sin could not atone;
Thou must save and thou alone:
In my hand no price I bring;
Simply to Thy cross I cling.

While I draw this fleeting breath,
When my eyes shall close in death,
When I rise to worlds unknown,
And behold Thee on Thy throne,
Rock of Ages, cleft for me,
Let me hide myself in Thee.

Augustus M. Toplady

OTHING to do but work,
　　Nothing to eat but food,
　　Nothing to wear but clothes
　　　To keep one from going nude.

Nothing to breathe but air,
　Quick as a flash it's gone;
Nowhere to fall but off,
　Nowhere to stand but on.

Nothing to comb but hair,
　Nowhere to sleep but bed,
Nothing to weep but tears,
　Nothing to bury but dead.

Nothing to sing but songs,
　Ah, well! Alas! Alack!
Nowhere to go but out,
　Nowhere to come but back.

Nothing to read but words,
　Nothing to cast but votes,
Nothing to hear but sounds,
　Nothing to sail but boats.

Nothing to see but sights,
　Nothing to quench but thirst,
Nothing to have but what we've got,
　Thus through life we are cursed.

Nothing to strike but a gait,
  Everything moves that goes.
Nothing at all but commonsense
  Can ever withstand these woes.

Ben King

⤙ A PSALM OF DAVID ⤚

THE LORD is my shepherd—
    I shall not want:
    He maketh me to lie down in green pastures;
    He leadeth me beside still waters.
He restoreth my soul;
    He guideth me in the paths of righteousness for His name's
    sake.
Yea, though I walk through the valley of the shadow of death
    I will fear no evil; for Thou art with me;
    Thy rod and Thy staff, they comfort me.
Thou preparest a table before me in the presence of mine ene-
    mies:
    Thou hast anointed my head with oil;
    My cup runneth over.
Only goodness and loving kindness shall follow me all the days
    of my life.
And I shall dwell in the house of my Lord for ever.

The Twenty-third Psalm
from THE BOOK OF PSALMS

[43]

s THE old year sinks down in Time's ocean,
 Stand ready to launch with the new,
And waste no regrets, no emotion,
 As the spars and the masts pass from view.
Weep not if some treasures go under,
 And sink in the other ship's hold—
That New Year that's sailing just yonder
 May bring you more good than the old.

For the world is forever improving—
 All the past is not worth one today—
And whatever deserves our true loving,
 Is stronger than death or decay.
Old love—was it wasted devotion?
 Old friends—were they weak or untrue?
Well, let them sink there in mid-ocean,
 And sail gaily on to the new.

Throw overboard useless regretting,
 Or deeds which you cannot undo,
And learn the great art of forgetting
 Old things which embitter the new.
Sing who will of dead years departed,
 I shroud them and bid them adieu;
And the song that I sing, happy-hearted,
 Is a song of the glorious new.

Ella Wheeler Wilcox

No single eye can measure the greatness of our country. But if you wanted a height on which to sit and look out over the nation, Pike's Peak would be a classic choice.

It was there a New England college teacher was inspired by the sweeping land below her to write the patriotic hymn, "America the Beautiful." It took several years to work it into the form we learned in school. But here, as an example of how the poem "gushed from the heart," is the first version—as it was published in "The Congregationalist" in 1895, on the Fourth of July.

O BEAUTIFUL for halcyon skies,
    For amber waves of grain,
    For purple mountain majesties
      Above the enameled plain!
  America! America!
  God shed his grace on thee
Till souls wax fair as earth and air
  And music-hearted sea!

O beautiful for pilgrim feet,
    Whose stern, impassioned stress
A thoroughfare for freedom beat
    Across the wilderness!
    America! America!
  God shed his grace on thee
Till paths be wrought through wilds of thought
  By pilgrim foot and knee!

O beautiful for glory-tale
   Of liberating strife,
When once and twice, for man's avail,
   Men lavished precious life!
     America! America!
   God shed his grace on thee
Till selfish gain no longer stain
   The banner of the free!

O beautiful for patriot dream
   That sees beyond the years
Thine alabaster cities gleam
   Undimmed by human tears!
     America! America!
   God shed his grace on thee,
Till nobler men keep once again
   Thy whiter jubilee!

Katharine Lee Bates

❧ MARRIAGE ❧

wo volumes bound in one, complete,
   A thrilling story old but sweet;
   No title needs the cover fair,
   Two golden hearts are blended there.

Mildred Merle

F I had known in the morning
How wearily all the day
The words unkind
Would trouble my mind
I said when you went away,
I had been more careful, darling
Nor given you needless pain;
But we vex our own
With look and tone
We might never take back again.

For though in the quiet evening
You may give me the kiss of peace,
Yet it might be
That never for me
The pain of the heart should cease.
How many go forth in the morning
That never come home at night,
And hearts have broken
For harsh words spoken
That sorrow can never set right.

We have careful thoughts for the stranger
And smiles for the sometime guest,
But oft for our own
This bitter tone,
Though we love our own the best.

Ah! lips with the curve impatient,
    Ah! brow with that look of scorn,
'T were a cruel fate
Were the night too late
    To undo the work of morn.

Margaret Elizabeth Sangster

❧ ASK AND YE SHALL RECEIVE ❧

 PRAYING ONE, who long has prayed,
    And yet no answer heard,
Have you been sometimes half afraid
    God might not keep His word?
Seems prayer to fall on deafened ears?
    Does Heaven seem blind and dumb?
Is hope deferred? Believe—believe—
    The answer time will come!

God heard you; He has not forgot;
    Faith shall at length prevail;
You know that not one smallest jot
    Of all His word can fail.
For if you truly have believed,
    Not vain has been your prayer!
As God is true, your answer comes—
    Sometime, someway, somewhere.

Mrs. Havens

[48]

ES, I know there are stains on my carpet,
  The traces of small muddy boots;
And I see your fair tapestry glowing,
  All spotless with flowers and fruits.

And I know that my walls are disfigured
  With prints of small fingers and hands;
And that your own household most truly
  In immaculate purity stands.

And I know that my parlor is littered
  With many odd treasures and toys,
While your own is in daintiest order,
  Unharmed by the presence of boys.

And I know that my room is invaded
  Quite boldly all hours of the day,
While you sit in yours unmolested
  And dream the soft quiet away.

Yes, I know there are those little bedsides
  Where I must stand watchful each night,
While you may go out in your carriage
  And flash in your dresses so bright.

Now, I think I'm a neat little woman;
  And I like my house orderly, too;
And I'm fond of all dainty belongings;
  But I would not change places with you.

No! Keep your fair home with its order,
　　Its freedom from bother and noise;
And keep your own fanciful leisure,
　　But give me my dear, splendid boys.

DREAMS

HO first said "False as dreams"? Not one who saw
　　Into the wild and wondrous world they sway—
No thinker who has read their mystic law,
　　No poet who has weaved them in his lay.

Else had he known that through the human breast
　　Cross and recross a thousand fleeting gleams
That, passed unnoticed in the day's unrest,
　　Come out at night, like stars, in shining dreams;

That minds too busy or too dull to mark
　　The dim suggestion of the noisier hours,
By dreams in the deep silence of the dark
　　Are roused at midnight with their folded powers.

Each has its lesson; for our dreams in sooth—
　　Come they in shape of demons, gods, or elves—
Are allegories with deep heart of truth
　　That tell us solemn secrets of ourselves.

Henry Timrod

Here is a classic example of the poem sprung from the heart. No critic would rank Elizabeth Barrett Browning above her husband, Robert Browning. But no poem of his is as well remembered as this one she wrote, out of the fullness of her love, to him.

ow DO I love you? Let me count the ways.
I love you to the depth and breadth and height
My soul can reach, when feeling out of sight
For the ends of Being and ideal Grace.
I love you to the level of everyday's
Most quiet need, by sun and candle-light.
I love you freely, as men strive for Right;
I love you purely, as they turn from Praise.
I love you with the passion put to use
In my old griefs, and with my childhood's faith.
I love you with a love I seemed to lose
With my lost saints. I love you with the breath,
Smiles, tears, of all my life! And, if God choose,
I shall but love you better after death.

Elizabeth Barrett Browning

EAD, kindly Light, amid the encircling gloom,
   Lead Thou me on!
The night is dark, and I am far from home—
   Lead Thou me on!
Keep Thou my feet; I do not ask to see
The distant scene—one step's enough for me.

I was not ever thus, nor prayed that Thou
   Shouldst lead me on.
I loved to choose and see my path; but now
   Lead Thou me on!
I loved the garish day, and spite of fears,
Pride ruled my will; remember not past years.

So long Thy power hath blest me, sure it still
   Will lead me on,
O'er moor and fen, o'er crag and torrent, till
   The night is gone;
And with the morn those angel faces smile
Which I have loved long since and lost awhile.

John Henry Cardinal Newman

✦ WHAT HAVE WE DONE ✦ TODAY?

E SHALL do so much in the years to come,
    But what have we done today?
    We shall give our gold in a princely sum,
    But what did we give today?
We shall lift the heart and dry the tear,
We shall plant a hope in the place of fear,
We shall speak the words of love and cheer,
    But what did we speak today?

We shall be so kind in the afterwhile,
    But what have we been today?
We shall bring each lonely life a smile,
    But what have we brought today?
We shall give to truth a grander birth,
And to steadfast faith a deeper worth,
We shall feed the hungering souls of earth,
    But whom have we fed today?

We shall reap such joys in the by-and-by,
    But what have we sown today?
We shall build us mansions in the sky,
    But what have we built today?
It's sweet in idle dreams to bask,
But here and now do we do our task?
Yes, this is the thing our souls must ask,
    What have we done today?

Nixon Waterman

[53]

MILE, and the world smiles with you;
   Knock, and you go it alone;
     For the cheerful grin
     Will let you in
Where the kicker is never known.

Growl, and the way looks dreary;
   Laugh, and the path is bright;
     For a welcome smile
     Brings sunshine, while
A frown shuts out the light.

Sigh, and you rake in nothing;
   Work, and the prize is won;
     For the nervy man
     With backbone can
By nothing be outdone.

Hustle, and fortune may bless you;
   Quit, and defeat is sure;
     For there's no chance
     Of deliverance
For the man who can't endure.

Sing, and the world's harmonious;
   Grumble, and things go wrong;
     And all the time
     You are out of rhyme
With the busy, bustling throng.

Kick, and there's trouble brewing;
　　Whistle, and life is gay—
　　　All the world's in tune
　　　Like a day in June,
　　And the clouds all melt away.

❧ CHARITY ❧

HERE IS so much that is bad in the best of us,
And so much that is good in the worst of us,
That it doesn't behoove any of us
To talk about the rest of us.

❧ SHAME ON ADAM ❧

HEN Eve upon the first of men
　　The apple pressed with specious cant,
　Oh! what a thousand pities then,
　　That Adam was not adamant.

SEND THEM TO BED
WITH A KISS

 MOTHERS, so weary, discouraged,
　　　Worn out with the cares of the day,
You often grow cross and impatient,
　　　Complain of the noise and the play;
For the day brings so many vexations,
　　So many things going amiss;
But, mothers, whatever may vex you,
　　Send the children to bed with a kiss!

The dear little feet wander often,
　　Perhaps, from the pathway of right,
The dear little hands find new mischief
　　To try you from morning till night;
But think of the desolate mothers
　　Who'd give all the world for your bliss,
And, as thanks for your infinite blessings,
　　Send the children to bed with a kiss!

For some day their noise will not vex you,
　　The silence will hurt you far more;
You will long for their sweet childish voices,
　　For a sweet childish face at the door;
And to feel a child's arms wrapped around you—
　　You'd give all the world for just this!
For the comfort it'll bring you tomorrow,
　　Send the children to bed with a kiss!

KNOW a funny little man,
   As quiet as a mouse,
Who does the mischief that is done
   In everybody's house!
There's no one ever sees his face,
  And yet we all agree
That every plate we break was cracked
  By Mr. Nobody.

It's he who always tears our books,
  Who leaves the door ajar,
He pulls the buttons from our shirts,
  And scatters pins afar;
That squeaking door will always squeak,
  For, really, don't you see,
We leave the oiling to be done
  By Mr. Nobody.

The finger marks upon the door
  By none of us are made;
We never leave the blinds unclosed,
  To let the curtains fade.
The ink we never spill; the shoes
  That lying 'round you see
Are not our shoes—they all belong
  To Mr. Nobody.

F ALL who hate would love us,
 And all our loves were true,
The stars that swing above us
 Would brighten in the blue.
If cruel words were kisses,
 And every scowl a smile,
A better world than this is,
 Would hardly be worth while.
If purses would not tighten
 To meet a brother's need,
The load we bear would lighten
 Above the grave of greed.

If those who whine would whistle,
 And those who languish laugh,
The rose would rout the thistle,
 The grain outrun the chaff.
If hearts were only jolly,
 If grieving were forgot,
And tears of melancholy
 Were things that now are not;
Then love would kneel to duty,
 And all the world would seem
A bridal bower of beauty,
 A dream within a dream.

If men would cease to worry,
   And women cease to sigh,
And all be glad to bury
   Whatever has to die;
If neighbor spoke to neighbor,
   As love demands of all,
The rust would eat the saber,
   The spear stay on the wall;
Then every day would glisten,
   And every eye would shine,
And God would pause to listen,
   And life would be divine.

James Newton Matthews

❧ LITTLE THINGS ☙

 ITTLE DROPS of water,
   Little grains of sand,
   Make a mighty ocean
   And the pleasant land.

Little deeds of kindness,
Little words of love,
Make this world an Eden
Like the world above.

Julia A. F. Carney

[59]

✣ LAUGH AND THE WORLD ✣
LAUGHS WITH YOU

LAUGH and the world laughs with you;
   Weep, and you weep alone;
   For this brave old earth must borrow its mirth,
   It has trouble enough of its own.
Sing and the hills will answer;
Sigh, it is lost on the air;
The echoes bound to a joyful sound,
But shrink from voicing care.

Rejoice, and men will seek you;
Grieve, and they turn and go;
They want full measure of all your pleasure,
But they do not want your woe.
Be glad, and your friends are many;
Be sad, and you lose them all—
There are none to decline your nectared wine,
But alone you must drink life's gall.

Feast and your halls are crowded;
Fast and the world goes by.
Succeed and give, and it helps you live,
But no man can help you die.
There is room in the halls of pleasure
For a long and lordly train;
So fill life to its greatest measure
And you'll never be alone again.

Ella Wheeler Wilcox

UST to be tender, just to be true,
Just to be glad the whole day through;
Just to be merciful, just to be mild—
Always as trustful as a child;
Just to be gentle and kind and sweet—
Just to be helpful with willing feet;
Just to be cheery when things go wrong,
Just to drive sadness away with song,
Just to be loyal and firm in right
Whether the hour is dark or bright;
Just to believe that God knows best,
Just in His promises ever to rest;
Just to let love be our daily key,
That is God's will for you and me.

❧ I SHALL NOT PASS AGAIN ❧ THIS WAY

 HE BREAD that gives men strength I want to give;
The water which the thirsting need to live:
I want to lift the faint who fall each day;
I'm sure I shall not pass again this way.

I want to give serenity for tears,
The faith to conquer crowding doubts and fears.
For ashes, beauty I would like to pay;
I'm sure I shall not pass again this way.

I want to give good measure running over,
And always help each angry heart discover
The answer soft that turneth wrath away;
I'm sure I shall not pass again this way.

I want to give strong hope, firm faith, and sweet,
Warm charity to all whom I may meet;
As God ordained I want to live each day;
I'm sure I shall not pass again this way.

Ellen H. Underwood

ঙ্গ MERCY ই৯

HE QUALITY of mercy is not strained:
It droppeth as the gentle rain from heaven
Upon the place beneath. It is twice blessed—
It blesses him that gives and him that takes.
'Tis mightiest in the mightiest: it becomes
The throned monarch better than his crown—
His sceptre shows the force of temporal power,
The attribute to awe and majesty
Wherein does sit the dread and fear of kings:
But mercy is above this sceptred sway;
It is enthroned in the hearts of kings—
It is an attribute to God himself;
And earthly power does then show like to God's
When mercy seasons justice.

William Shakespeare

[62]

HE captains and chiefs are all wedded, I guess—
  The leaders, the rich and the great;
Their wives, I suppose, all enjoy their success
  And dote on each triumphing mate.

And you, I know well, have strived hard to be there
  Front-ranked with the leaders of men,
But I am content that you are not, my dear,
  For what would our life be like then?

If maids did your bidding and cleaned up the house,
  And you had a chef or cook, too,
Then what would you need of your fond little spouse?
  Why, you'd never enjoy a good stew!

If we had the money to buy all the gowns,
  No new dress could give me much pleasure;
If all of your life were just up and no downs,
  Then how could you take my love's measure?

So men may not run at your order or word
  Passed down from some height far above,
But what could you say that's as great as I've heard
  In your whispers to me of our love?

Martina Foley

Poetry has largely ignored the drama of the elderly.

This rare poem etches sharply the poignancy of advancing years when the veil between here and hereafter is worn thin by time, basing it on the last days of St. John the Evangelist—the "beloved disciple" pictured with his head on Jesus' heart in the Last Supper scene—the one apostle who escaped martyrdom and lived on to his 99th year.

I'M GROWING very old. This weary head
That hath so often leaned on Jesus' breast,
In days long past that seem almost a dream,
Is bent and hoary with its weight of years.

These limbs that followed Him, My Master, oft
From Galilee to Judah—yea, that stood
Beneath the Cross and trembled with His groans—
Refuse to bear me even through the streets
To preach unto my children.

               E'en my lips
Refuse to form the words my heart sends forth.
My ears are dull; they scarcely hear the sobs
Of my dear children gathered 'round my couch;
My eyes so dim, they cannot see their tears.

God lays His hand upon me—yea, His hand,
And not His rod—the gentle hand that I
Felt, those three years, so often pressed in mine,
In friendship such as passeth woman's love.

I'm old, so old! I cannot recollect
The faces of my friends and I forget
The words and deeds that make up daily life:
But that dear Face, and every word He spoke,
Grow more distinct as others fade away,
So that I live with Him and th' holy dead
More than with living . . .

. . . Oh! how oft I've seen
The touching of His garments bring back strength
To palsied limbs! I feel it has to mine.
Up! Bear me once more to my church—once more!
There let me tell them of a Savior's love;
For by the sweetness of my Master's voice
Just now, I think He must be very near—
Coming, I trust, to break the veil which time
Has worn so thin that I can see beyond,
And watch His footsteps . . .

. . . O, my Lord! my Lord!
How bright Thou art, and yet the very same
I loved in Galilee! 'Tis worth the hundred years
To feel this bliss! So lift me up, dear Lord,
Unto Thy bosom, full of perfect peace.

OBODY knows of the work it makes
    To keep the home together,
Nobody knows of the steps it takes,
    Nobody knows—but mother.

Nobody listens to childish woes,
    Which kisses only smother;
Nobody's pained by naughty blows,
    Nobody—only mother.

Nobody knows of the sleepless care
    Bestowed on baby brother;
Nobody knows of the tender prayer,
    Nobody—only mother.

Nobody knows of the lessons taught
    Of loving one another;
Nobody knows of the patience sought,
    Nobody—only mother.

Nobody knows of the anxious fears,
    Lest darlings may not weather
The storm of life in after years,
    Nobody knows—but mother.

Nobody kneels at the throne above
    To thank the Heavenly Father
For that sweetest gift—a mother's love;
    Nobody can—but mother.

·§ IF YOU HAVE A FRIEND ·€
WORTH LOVING

F YOU have a friend worth loving,
  Love him. Yes, and let him know
That you love him, ere life's evening
  Tinge his brow with sunset glow.
Why should good words not be said
Of a friend till he is dead?

If you hear a song that thrills you,
  Sung by any child of song,
Praise it. Do not let the singer
  Wait deserved praises long.
Why should one who thrills your heart
Lack the joy you may impart?

If you hear a prayer that moves you
  By its humble, pleading tone,
Join it. Do not let the seeker
  Bow before his God alone.
Why should not your brother share
The strength of "two or three" in prayer?

If you see the hot tears falling
  From a brother's weeping eyes,
Share them; and by kindly sharing
  Own your kinship in the skies.
Why should anyone be glad
When a brother's heart is sad?

If a silvery laugh goes rippling
    Through the sunshine on his face,
Share it. It's the wise man's saying—
    For both grief and joy a place.
There's health and goodness in the mirth
In which an honest laugh has birth.

If your work is made more easy
    By a friendly, helping hand,
Say so. Speak out bravely, truly,
    Or a dark may veil the land.
Should a brother workman near,
Falter for a word of cheer?

Scatter thus your seeds of kindness
    All enriching as you go—
Leave them. Trust the Harvest-Giver;
    He will make each seed to grow.
And, until the happy end,
Your life shall never lack a friend.

❧ LIFE SCULPTURE ❧

CHISEL in hand stood a sculptor-boy
    With his marble block before him,
And his face lit up with a smile of joy,
    As an angel-dream passed o'er him.
He carved the dream on that shapeless stone
    With many a sharp incision;
With heaven's own light the sculpture shone—
    He'd caught that angel-vision!

Sculptors of life are we, as we stand
  With our souls uncarved before us,
Waiting the hour when, at God's command,
  Our life-dream shall pass o'er us.
If we carve it then on the yielding stone
  With many a sharp incision,
Its heavenly beauty shall be our own—
  Our lives—the angel-vision.

George W. Doane

◆§ TRUE REST §◆

EST is not quitting
    The busy career;
Rest is the fitting
    Of self to one's sphere:

As the brook's motion,
  Full of strong life,
Flows to the ocean—
  Calm, without strife.

Loving and serving
  All that is best,
Onward, unswerving,
  This is true rest.

Johann Wolfgang von Goethe

[69]

ULL many a blessing wears the guise
    Of worry or of trouble;
    Far-seeing is the soul, and wise,
      Who knows the mask is double.
And he who has the faith and strength
   To thank his God for sorrow,
Has found a joy without alloy
   To gladden every morrow.

There's not a day in all the year
   But holds some hidden pleasure;
And looking back, joys oft appear
   To brim the past's wide measure.
But blessings are like friends, I hold,
   Who love and labor near us,
We ought to raise our notes of praise
   While living hearts can hear us.

We ought to make the moments notes
   Of happy, glad Thanksgiving,
The hours and days a silent phrase
   Of music we are living.
And so the theme should swell and grow,
   As weeks and months pass o'er us,
And rise sublime at this good time
   In grand Thanksgiving chorus.

Ella Wheeler Wilcox

IFE, believe, is not a dream,
    So dark as sages say;
    Oft a little morning rain
    Foretells a pleasant day.
Sometimes there are clouds of gloom,
  But these are transient all;
If the shower will make the roses bloom,
  Oh, why lament its fall?
    Rapidly, merrily,
  Life's sunny hours flit by;
    Gratefully, cheerily,
Enjoy them as they fly.

What though Death at times steps in,
  And calls our Best away?
What though Sorrow seems to win,
  O'er Hope a heavy sway?
Yet Hope again elastic springs,
  Unconquered, though she fell;
Still buoyant are her golden wings,
  Still strong to bear us well.
    Manfully, fearlessly,
  The day of trial bear,
    For gloriously, victoriously,
Can courage quell despair!

Charlotte Brontë

Not long ago, Americans' roots reached across a sea or from city back to farm. More commonly today, "back home" means another state. "Poet-Ranchman" Chittenden was an early example of this. He wrote equally from his heart of Texas and New Jersey. This Chittenden poem about the Texas we all know from books, films and television, is for all those with roots elsewhere— as a voice from "back home."

He's a quiet, easy fellow, with his pants tucked in his boots,
And he wears a big revolver which he seldom ever shoots;
He has served his time as Ranger on the reckless Rio Grande,
And he has the reputation for great marksmanship and sand;
He has strung up several horse thieves in the rustler days gone by,
And although he seems so pleasant there's a devil in his eye.

When he goes to take a prisoner, he calls him by his name,
In that confidential manner which suggests the bunco game;
If the culprit is not willing, takes exception to the plan,
Our Sheriff gets the drop, sir, and he likewise gets his man.
"Here's looking at you, Sheriff!"—come, boys, let's drink her down
To the most important man, sir, of every Texas town.

Larry Chittenden

[72]

EARER, my God, to Thee,
   Nearer to Thee!
E'en though it be a cross
   That raiseth me;
Still all my song shall be,
Nearer, my God, to Thee,
   Nearer to Thee!

Though like the wanderer,
   The sun gone down,
Darkness be over me,
   My rest a stone—
Yet in my dreams I'd be
Nearer, my God, to Thee,
   Nearer to Thee!

There let the way appear,
   Steps unto heaven;
All that Thou sendest me
   In mercy given;
Angels to beckon me
Nearer, my God, to Thee,
   Nearer to Thee!

Then, with my waking thoughts
   Bright with Thy praise,
Out of my stony griefs,

Bethel I'll raise,
So by my woes to be
Nearer, my God, to Thee,
  Nearer to Thee!

Or if, on joyful wing,
  Cleaving the sky,
Sun, moon and stars forgot,
  Upward I fly;
Still all my song shall be,
Nearer, my God, to Thee,
  Nearer to Thee!

Sarah Flower Adams

DANDELIONS

HERE surely is a gold mine somewhere underneath the
        grass,
    For dandelions are popping out in every place you
        pass.
But if you want to gather some you'd better not delay,
For the gold will turn to silver soon and all will blow away.

THE IDEAL HUSBAND
TO HIS WIFE

E'VE lived for many years, dear wife,
   And walked together side by side,
And you today are just as dear
   As when you were my bride.
I've tried to make life glad for you—
   One long, sweet honeymoon of joy,
A dream of marital content
   Without the least alloy.
I've smoothed all boulders from our path,
   That we, in peace, might toil along,
By always hastening to admit
   That I was right and you were wrong.

No mad diversity of creed
   Has ever sundered you from me;
For I permit you evermore
   To take all your ideas from me.
And well I know our marriage bliss
   While life shall last will never cease;
For I shall always let you do,
   In generous love, just what I please.
Peace comes, and discord flies away,
   Love's bright day follows hatred's night;
For I am ready to admit
   That you are wrong and I am right.

Sam Walter Foss

ow OFTEN passing words will tend
In visions to recall
Our truest, dearest, fondest friend—
That earliest friend of all.

Who tended on our childish years—
Those years that pass as hours,
When all earth's dewy, trembling tears
Lie hid within her flowers.

You star that shines in darkest night,
When most we need your aid,
Unchanging but to beam more bright
When others coldly fade.

Oh, Mother! 'round your happy name
Such blissful memory springs:
The heart in all but years the same,
With reverent worship clings.

Your voice was first to hail us, when
We first knew victory:
And if our hopes were crushed down, then
Your love was sympathy.

A PSALM OF LIFE

ELL ME not in mournful numbers,
    Life is but an empty dream!
For the soul is dead that slumbers,
    Things are not just as they seem.

Life is real! Life is earnest!
    And the grave is not its goal;
"Dust thou art, to dust returnest,"
    Was not spoken of the soul.

Not enjoyment and not sorrow,
    Is our destined end or way;
But to act that each tomorrow
    Find us further than today.

Art is long, and time is fleeting,
    And our hearts, though stout and brave,
Still, like muffled drums, are beating
    Funeral marches to the grave.

In the world's broad field of battle,
    In the bivouac of life,
Be not like dumb, driven cattle!
    Be a hero in the strife!

Trust no future, howe'er pleasant!
    Let the dead past bury its dead!
Act, act in the living present!
    Heart within, God overhead!

[77]

Lives of great men all remind us
    We can make our lives sublime,
And, departing, leave behind us
    Footprints on the sands of time.

Footprints, that perhaps another
    Broken in life's daily strain—
Some forlorn and shipwrecked brother—
    Seeing, shall take heart again.

Let us then, be up and doing,
    With a heart for any fate;
Still achieving, still pursuing,
    Learn to labor and to wait.

Henry Wadsworth Longfellow

✑ TODAY! ✑

 ITH every rising of the sun,
    Think of your life as just begun.
    The past has cancelled and buried deep
    All yesterdays. There let them sleep.
Concern yourself with just today.
Grasp it, and teach it to obey
Your will and plan. Since time began
Today has been the friend of man.
Today and you! Your soul sublime
And this great heritage of time,
With God himself to bind the two.
Go forth, brave heart: today's for you!

T LOOKED extremely rocky for the Mudville nine that
day:
The score stood four to six with but an inning left to
play.
And so, when Cooney died at first, and Burrows did the same,
A pallor wreathed the features of the patrons of the game.

A straggling few got up to go, leaving there the rest
With that hope which springs eternal within the human breast.
For they thought if only Casey could get a whack at that,
They'd put up even money with Casey at the bat.

But Flynn preceded Casey and likewise so did Blake,
And the former was a nothing and the latter was a fake;
So on that stricken multitude a death-like silence sat,
For there seemed but little chance of Casey's getting to the bat.

But Flynn let drive a single to the wonderment of all,
And the fake whom they called Blakey tore the cover off the ball.
And when the dust had lifted and they saw what had occurred,
There was Blakey safe on second, and Flynn was hugging third.

Then from the gladdened multitude went up a joyous yell,
It bounded from the mountain-top and rattled in the dell,
It struck upon the hillside, and rebounded on the flat,
For Casey, mighty Casey, was advancing to the bat.

There was ease in Casey's manner as he stepped into his place;
There was pride in Casey's bearing and a smile on Casey's face.
And when, responding to the cheers, he lightly doffed his hat,
No stranger in the crowd could doubt, 'twas Casey at the bat.

Ten thousand eyes were on him as he rubbed his hands with dirt,
Five thousand tongues applauded as he wiped them on his shirt;
And while the writhing pitcher ground the ball into his hip,
Defiance gleamed from Casey's eye—a sneer curled Casey's lip.

And now the leather-covered sphere came hurtling through the
    air,
But Casey stood and watched it pass—in haughty grandeur there.
Close by the sturdy batter the ball unheeded sped.
"That ain't my style," said Casey. "Strike one!" the umpire said.

From the grandstand black with people there rose a sullen roar,
Like the beating of the storm waves on a stern and distant shore:
"Kill him! Kill the umpire!" some one shouted from the stand—
And it's likely they'd have done it had not Casey raised his hand.

With a smile of Christian charity great Casey's visage shone;
He stilled the rising tumult and he bade the game go on.
He signalled to the pitcher and again the spheroid flew,
But Casey still ignored it and the umpire said, "Strike two!"

"Fraud!" yelled the maddened thousands, and the echo an-
    swered, "Fraud!"
But one scornful look from Casey and the audience was awed.
They saw his face grow stern and cold, they saw his muscles
    strain:
They knew that Casey would not let that ball go by again.

The sneer is gone from Casey's lip; his teeth are clenched with
 hate;
He pounds with cruel violence his bat upon the plate.
And now the pitcher holds the ball; and now he lets it go—
And now the air is shattered by the force of Casey's blow.

Oh! Somewhere in this favored land the sun is shining bright,
The band is playing somewhere, and somewhere hearts are light;
And somewhere men are laughing, and somewhere children
 shout:
But there is no joy in Mudville—mighty Casey has struck out.

Ernest Lawrence Thayer

⁊ A BIRTHDAY GIFT ⁊
AT CHRISTMAS

HAT can I give Him,
 Poor as I am?
If I were a shepherd
 I would bring a lamb;
If I were a Wise Man
I would do my part—
Yet what can I give Him?
 Give my heart.

Christina Georgina Rossetti

E WILL be what we could be. Do not say,
    "It might have been, had not or that, or this."
No fate can keep us from the chosen way;
    He only might, who is.

We will do what we could do. Do not dream
    Chance leaves a hero, all uncrowned to grieve.
I hold all men are greatly what they seem;
    He does, who could achieve.

We will climb where we could climb. Tell me not
    Of adverse storms that keep you from the height.
What eagle ever missed the peak he sought?
    He always climbs who might.

I do not like the phrase, "It might have been!"
    It lacks all force, and life's best truth perverts:
For I believe we have, and reach, and win,
    Whatever our deserts.

Ella Wheeler Wilcox

Milton's towering reputation as a poet overshadows the fact that he was an important propagandist for the Puritan revolution in England, and an important public official under Cromwell. The onset of his blindness not only handicapped him as a writer and reduced his ability to function as a public officer but—according to the Puritan ethic of which he was an ardent apostle—threatened his very soul: he who could not work to the limit could not hope to win Heaven. It was in the furnace of that frightful quandary that his powerful mind and pen fused to produce this sonnet.

HEN I consider how my life is spent
Ere half my days, in this dark world and wide,
And that one talent which is death to hide
Lodged with me useless, though my soul more bent
To serve therewith my Maker, and present
My true account, lest He returning chide—
Doth God exact day-labor, light denied?
I fondly ask. But Patience, to prevent
That murmur, soon replies: God doth not need
Either man's work, or His own gifts; who best
Bear His mild yoke—they serve Him best. His state
Is kingly: thousands at His bidding speed
And post o'er land and ocean without rest.
They also serve who only stand and wait.

John Milton

[83]

❧ THE SUNRISE NEVER ❧
FAILED US YET

PON the sadness of the sea
The sunset broods regretfully;
From the far, lonely places, slow
Withdraws the wistful afterglow.

So out of life the splendor dies;
So darken all the happy skies;
So gathers twilight, cold and stern:
But overhead the planets burn.

And up the East another day
Shall chase the dismal dark away;
What though our eyes with tears be wet?
The sunrise never failed us yet.

The blush of dawn may yet restore
Our light and hope and joy once more.
Sad soul, take comfort, nor forget
That sunrise never failed us yet!

Celia Thaxter

⊰ LET SOMETHING GOOD ⊱
BE SAID

HEN over the fair fame of friend or foe
     The shadow of disgrace shall fall; instead
Of words of blame, or proof of so-and-so,
     Let something good be said.

Forget not that no fellow-being yet
     May fall so low but love may lift his head;
Even the cheek of shame with tears is wet,
     If something good be said.

No generous heart may vainly turn aside
     In ways of sympathy; no soul so dead
But may awaken strong and glorified,
     If something good be said.

And so I charge you, by the thorny crown,
     And by the cross on which the Savior bled,
And by your own soul's hope for fair renown,
     Let something good be said.

James Whitcomb Riley

WAY to and fro in the twilight gray;
    This is the ferry for Shadowtown;
It always sails at the end of day,
    Just as the darkness closes down.

Rest, little head, on my shoulder, so;
    A sleepy kiss is the only fare;
Drifting away from the world, we go,
    Baby and I in the rocking chair.

See where the fire-logs glow and spark,
    Glitter the lights of the shadow-land,
The raining drops on the window, hark!
    Are ripples lapping upon its strand.

There, where the mirror is glancing dim,
    A lake lies shimmering, cool and still.
Blossoms are waving above its brim,
    Those over there on the window-sill.

Rock slow, more slow in the dusky light,
    Silently lower the anchor down:
Dear little passenger, say "Good-night"
    We've reached the harbor of Shadowtown.

[86]

OMETIME, when all life's lessons have been learned,
 And sun and stars forevermore have set,
The things which our weak judgment here have
  spurned,
The things o'er which we grieved with lashes wet,
Will flash before us, out of life's dark night,
 As stars shine more in deeper tints of blue,
And we shall see how all God's plans were right,
 And how what seemed reproof was love most true.

And we shall see how, while we frown and sigh,
 God's plans go on as best for you and me;
How, when we called, He heeded not our cry,
 Because His wisdom to the end could see.
And even as prudent parents disallow
 Too much of sweet to craving babyhood,
So God, perhaps, is keeping from us now
 Life's sweetest things, because for us it's good.

And if, sometimes commingled with life's wine,
 We find the wormwood and rebel and shrink,
Be sure a wiser hand than yours or mine
 Pours out this potion for our lips to drink.
And if some friend we love is lying low,
 Where human kisses cannot reach his face,
Oh, do not blame the loving Father so!
 But wear your sorrow with obedient grace.

And you shall shortly know that lengthened breath
   Is not the sweetest gift God sends His friend,
And that sometimes the sable pall of death
   Conceals the fairest boon His love can send.
If we could push ajar the gates of life
   And stand within and all God's workings see,
We could interpret all this doubt and strife,
   And for each mystery could find a key.

But not today. Then be content, poor heart!
   God's plans, like lilies, pure and white unfold.
We must not tear the close-shut leaves apart;
   Time will reveal the hidden cups of gold.
And if through patient toil we reach the land,
   Where weary feet, with sandals loosed, may rest,
Then shall we know and clearly understand—
   I think that we shall say, "God knows the best."

Mary Louise Riley Smith

❧ TRUTH, THE INVINCIBLE ❧

RUTH crushed to earth shall rise again—
   The eternal years of God are hers;
But Error, wounded, writhes with pain,
   And dies among his worshippers.

William Cullen Bryant

ET OTHERS sing to the hero who wins in the ceaseless
    fray,
    Who, over the crushed and fallen, pursues his up-
      ward way;
For him let them weave the laurel, to him be the paean sung,
Whom the kindly fates have chosen, who are happy their loved
    among;
But mine is a different message, some soul in its stress to reach;
To bind on the wounds of failure, the balm of pitying speech;
To whisper: "Be up and doing, for courage at last prevails"—
I sing—who have supped with Failure—I sing to the man who
    fails.

I know how the gray cloud darkens, and mantles the soul in
    gloom;
I know how the spirit harkens to voices of doubt or of doom;
I know how the tempter mutters his terrible word, "Despair!"
But the heart has its secret chamber, and I know that our God
    is there.
Our years are as moments only; our failures He counts as
    naught;
The stone that the builders rejected, perchance is the one that
    He sought.
Mayhap, in the ultimate judgment, the effort alone avails,
And the laurel of great achievement shall be for the man who
    fails.

We sow in the darkness only; but the Reaper shall reap in light;
And the day of His perfect glory shall tell of the deeds of the
  night.
We gather our gold, and store it, and the whisper is heard,
  "Success!"
But, tell me, you cold, white sleepers, what were an achievement
  less?
We struggle for fame, and win it; and lo! like a fleeting breath,
It is lost in the realm of silence whose ruler and king is Death.
Where are the Norseland heroes, the ghosts of a housewife's
  tales?
I sing—for the Father heeds him—I sing to the man who fails.

Oh, men, who are labelled "failures," up! rise up, again, and do!
Somewhere in the world of action is room; there is room for you.
No failure was ever recorded, in the annals of truthful men,
Except of the craven who failed and would not make a try again.
The glory is in the doing, and not in the trophy won;
The walls that are laid in darkness may laugh to the kiss of the
  sun;
Oh, weary and worn and stricken, oh, child of fate's cruel gales!
I sing—that it haply may cheer him—I sing to the man who fails.

Alfred J. Waterhouse

MOTHERS are the queerest things!
    Take that day John went away:
  All but mother cried and cried
    When they said good-bye that day.
She just talked, and seemed to be
  Not the slightest bit upset—
Was the only one who smiled!
  Others' eyes were streaming wet.

But when John came back again
  On a furlough, safe and sound,
With a medal for his deeds,
  And without a single wound,
While the rest of us hurrahed,
  Laughed and joked and danced about,
Mother kissed him, then she cried—
  Cried and cried like all get out!

Edwin L. Sabin

I F WE knew the cares and crosses
　　Crowding 'round our neighbor's way,
If we knew his little losses,
　　Sorely grievous day by day,
Would we then so often chide him
　For his lack of thrift and gain?
Casting on his life a shadow,
　Leaving on his heart a stain?

If we knew the silent story
　Quivering through some hearts of pain,
Would our human hearts dare doom them
　Back to haunts of guilt again?
Life has many a tangled crossing,
　Joy has many a change to woe;
And the cheeks tear-washed are whitest,
　As the blessed angels know.

Let us reach into our hearts, then,
　For the key to others' lives,
And with love to erring nature,
　Cherish good that still survives;
So that when our disrobed spirits
　Soar to realms of light again,
We may say, dear Father, judge us
　As we judged our fellowmen.

CRADLE HYMN

AWAY in a manger, no crib for a bed,
The little Lord Jesus laid down His sweet head.
The stars in the bright sky looked down
where He lay:
The little Lord Jesus asleep on the hay.

The cattle are lowing, the Baby awakes—
But little Lord Jesus, no crying He makes.
I love Thee, Lord Jesus! Look down from the sky
And stay by my cradle till morning is nigh.

Martin Luther

YOUR MISSION

IF YOU cannot on the ocean
Sail among the swiftest fleet
Rocking on the highest billows,
Laughing at the storms you meet,
You can stand among the sailors,
Anchored yet within the bay,
You can lend a hand to help them
As they launch their boats away.

[93]

If you are too weak to journey
    Up the mountain, steep and high,
You can stand within the valley
    While the multitudes go by;
You can chant in happy measure
    As they slowly pass along—
Though they may forget the singer,
    They will not forget the song.

If you have not gold and silver
    Ever ready at command;
If you cannot toward the needy
    Reach an ever-helping hand,
You can succor the afflicted,
    For the erring you can weep;
With the Savior's true disciples
    You a tireless watch may keep.

If you cannot in the harvest
    Gather up the richest sheaves,
Many a grain, both ripe and golden,
    Oft the careless reaper leaves;
Go and glean among the briers
    Growing rank against the wall,
For it may be that their shadow
    Hides the heaviest wheat of all.

Do not, then, stand idly waiting
    For some greater work to do;
Fortune is a lazy goddess—
    She will never come to you.

Go and toil in any vineyard;
    Do not fear to do or dare—
If you want a field of labor
    You can find it anywhere.

Ellen M. H. Gates

⊷ SOUVENIR ⊶

FOUND them in a book last night—
    These withered violets,
A token of that early love
    One never quite forgets.
Pressed carefully between the leaves,
    They keep their color still;
I cannot look at them today
    Without an old-time thrill.

Ah me, what tricks does memory play!
    The passing years have fled
And hopes that lived in vigor once,
    Alas! have long been dead.
And this is all that I can say,
    When all is said and done,
Those flowers remind me of some boy—
    I wish I knew which one!

I HAVE a little shadow that goes in and out with me,
And what can be the use of him is more than I can see.
He is very, very like me from the heels up to the head;
And I see him jump before me, when I jump into my
bed.

The funniest thing about him is the way he likes to grow—
Not at all like proper children, which is always very slow;
For he sometimes shoots up taller like an India-rubber ball,
And he sometimes gets so little that there's none of him at all.

He hasn't got a notion of how children ought to play,
And can only make a fool of me in every sort of way.
He stays so close beside me, he's a coward you can see;
I'd think shame to stick to mama as that shadow sticks to me!

One morning, very early, before the sun was up,
I rose and found the shining dew on every buttercup;
But my lazy little shadow, like an arrant sleepyhead,
Had stayed at home behind me and was fast asleep in bed.

Robert Louis Stevenson

KEEP pushing—it's wiser
    Than sitting aside
And dreaming and sighing
    And 'waiting the tide.
In life's earnest battle
    They only prevail
Who daily march onward
    And never say fail!

With an eye ever open,
    A tongue that's not dumb,
And a heart that will never
    To sorrow succumb,
You'll battle and conquer,
    Though thousands assail—
How strong and how mighty
    Who never say fail!

Ahead, then, keep pushing,
    And stick to your way,
Unheeding the envious,
    And asses who bray.
All obstacles vanish,
    All enemies quail,
In the might of their wisdom
    Who never say fail!

In life, as a child and
  In manhood's firm pride,
Let this be your motto
  Your footsteps to guide:
In storm and in sunshine,
  Whatever assail,
Move onward and conquer,
  And never say fail!

❧ THERE ARE LOYAL HEARTS ❧

HERE are loyal hearts, there are spirits brave,
  There are souls that are pure and true;
Then give to the world the best you have,
  And the best shall come back to you.

Give love, and love to your heart will flow,
  A strength in your utmost need;
Have faith, and a score of hearts will show
  Their faith in your word and deed.

For life is the mirror of king and slave,
  It's just what you are and do;
So give to the world the best you have,
  And the best will come back to you.

Madeline S. Bridges

MID the cares of married life,
In spite of toil and business strife,
If you value your sweet wife,
    Tell her so!

Prove to her you don't forget
The bond to which your seal is set;
Of all life's sweet, she's sweetest yet—
    Tell her so!

When days are dark and deeply blue,
She has her troubles, same as you;
Show her that your love is true—
    Tell her so!

In former days you praised her style,
And spent much care to win her smile;
It's just as well now worth your while—
    Tell her so!

There was a time you thought it bliss
To get the favor of one kiss;
A dozen now won't come amiss—
    Tell her so!

Your love for her is no mistake—
You feel it dreaming or awake—
Do not conceal it—for her sake.
    Tell her so!

You are hers, and hers alone—
Well you know she's all your own—
Don't wait to carve it on a stone;
    Tell her so!

Never let her heart grow cold—
Richer beauties will unfold;
She is worth her weight in gold!
    Tell her so!

⊰ SOMEBODY ⊱

OMEBODY did a golden deed;
    Somebody proved a friend in need;
    Somebody sang a beautiful song;
    Somebody smiled the whole day long;
Somebody thought, "Tis sweet to live;"
Somebody said, "I'm glad to give;"
Somebody fought a valiant fight;
Somebody lived to shield the right;
    Was that "somebody" you?

HO FED me from her gentle breast
And hushed me in her arms to rest,
And on my cheek sweet kisses pressed?
    My mother.

When sleep forsook my open eye,
Who was it sang sweet lullaby
And rocked me so I would not cry?
    My mother.

When pain and sickness made me cry,
Who gazed upon my heavy eye
And wept, for fear that I should die?
    My mother.

Who ran to help me when I fell
And would some pretty story tell,
Or kiss the place to make it well?
    My mother.

Who taught my infant lips to pray,
To love God's holy word and day,
And walk in wisdom's pleasant way?
    My mother.

How can I ever cease to be
Affectionate and kind to thee
Who was so very kind to me—
    My mother?

When you are feeble, old and gray,
My healthy arm shall be your stay,
And I will soothe your pains away,
    My mother.

And when I see you hang your head,
'Twill be my turn to watch your bed,
And tears of sweet affection shed—
    My mother.

Jane Taylor

❧ IMPRESSIONABLE ☙

 AY I print a kiss on your lips?" I asked.
  She nodded her sweet permission;
So we went to press, and I rather guess
  We printed a large edition.

❦ "TO KNOW ALL IS TO ❧ FORGIVE ALL"

F I KNEW you and you knew me—
    If both of us could clearly see,
    And with an inner sight divine
    The meaning of your heart and mine,
I'm sure that we would differ less
And clasp our hands in friendliness;
Our thoughts would pleasantly agree—
If I knew you and you knew me.

If I knew you and you knew me,
As each one knows his own self, we
Could look each other in the face
And see therein a truer grace.
Life has so many hidden woes,
So many thorns for every rose;
The "why" of things our hearts would see,
If I knew you and you knew me.

Nixon Waterman

F you tried and have not won,
 Never stop for crying;
All that's great and good is done
 Just by patient trying.

Though young birds, in flying, fall,
 Still their wings grow stronger;
And the next time they can stay
 Up a little longer.

Though the sturdy oak has known
 Many a blast that bowed her,
She has risen again, and grown
 Loftier and prouder.

If by easy work you beat
 Others, who will prize you?
Gaining victory from defeat—
 That's the test that tries you!

Phoebe Cary

EAR JACK," said Kate, with eyes of blue,
"To tell the truth I cannot see
Why you don't make a verse or two
Which I may say is all for me?"

"My love," said Jack, "that would I do,
If I did not with fear foresee
That if I made a verse to you,
It might make you averse to me."

❧ FROST PICTURES ❧

ICTURES on the window,
 Painted by Jack Frost
Coming at the midnight,
 With the noon are lost:
Here, a row of fir trees
 Standing straight and tall;
There a rapid river
 And a waterfall.

Here a branch of coral
 From the briny sea;
There a weary traveler
 Resting near a tree.

Thus a breath—the lightest—
  Resting in the air,
Jack Frost catches quickly
  And implants it there.

And thus you are painting,
  Little children, too,
On your life's fair window
  Always something new.
But your little pictures
  Will not pass away
Like those Jack Frost's fingers
  Paint each winter day.

Each kind word or action
  Is a picture bright;
Every duty mastered
  Is lovely, in the light.
Let the lines be always
  Made by kindness bright;
Paint your glass with pictures
  Of the true and right.

Alice Williams Brotherton

❧ FOR ALL THESE ❧

I THANK THEE, Lord, that I am straight and strong,
 With wit to work and hope to keep me brave;
That two score years, unfathomed, still belong
 To the allotted life Thy bounty gave.

I thank Thee that the sight of sunlit lands
 And dipping hills, the breath of evening grass—
That wet, dark rocks and flowers in my hands
 Can give me daily gladness as I pass.

I thank Thee that I love the things of earth—
 Ripe fruits and laughter, lying down to sleep,
The shine of lighted towns, the graver worth
 Of beating human hearts that laugh and weep.

I thank Thee that as yet I need not know,
 And need not fear the mystery of the end;
But more than all, and though all these should go—
 Dear Lord, this on my knees!—I thank Thee for my friend.

Juliet Wilbor Tompkins

HE HEAD is stately, calm and wise,
  And bears a princely part;
And down below in secret lies
  The warm, impulsive heart.

The lordly head that sits above,
  The heart that beats below,
Their differences plainly prove
  Their true relation show.

The head, erect, serene and cool,
  Endowed with reason's art,
Was set aloft to guide and rule
  The throbbing, wayward heart.

And from the head as from the higher,
  Comes every glorious thought;
And in the heart's transforming fire
  All noble deeds are wrought.

Yet each is best when both unite
  To make the man complete;
What were the heat without the light?
  The light, without the heat?

J. G. Saxe

WHEN you wake up in the morning of a chill and
    cheerless day,
      And feel inclined to grumble, pout, or frown,
    Just glance into your mirror and you will quickly see
It's just because the corners of your mouth turn down.

    Then take this simple rhyme,
    Remember it in time:
It's always dreary weather, in countryside or town,
When you wake and find the corners of your mouth turned
   down.

If you wake up in the morning full of bright and happy thoughts
   And begin to count the blessings in your cup,
Then glance into your mirror and you will quickly see
   It's all because the corners of your mouth turn up.

    Then take this little rhyme,
    Remember all the time:
There's joy a-plenty in this world to fill life's silver cup
If you'll only keep the corners of your mouth turned up.

Leila Linton

BEAUTIFUL babe in her cradle bed lay;
Her age might be reckoned by less than a day.
Two fairies stood watching her tiny clenched fist,
And rose-bud mouth that the angels had kissed.

Said one to the other, "What fairer abode
Could Heaven, in its bounty, on us have bestowed?"
Said the other: "None fairer; I claim her my own
By right of discovery: I came here alone."

"Ah, no," said the first, "that cannot be true,
Since no one denies I'm the shadow of you."
"I came here alone!" "Nay, I stood by your side."
"I will dwell in her lips." "In her heart I will hide."

The Smile wreathed her lips, falling slightly apart.
The Sigh sank in sadness down into her heart.
This was ages ago; how long I forget;
But the Smile and the Sigh strive for mastery yet.

G. T. Johnson

There are few Americans who don't know, and don't appreciate, the refrain of this song, written originally as part of an American opera. Possibly the poet's own wandering existence gave these lines the feeling which made them live.

It is an irony only a tragic poet could have conceived that the author died far from home, in Tunis, in Africa.

ID PLEASURES and palaces though we may roam,
Be it ever so humble, there's no place like home:
A charm from above seems to hallow us there,
Which, seek through the world, is not met with elsewhere.
  Home! Home! Sweet, sweet home!
  There's no place like home—
  No, there's no place like home!

If home I'd return, overburdened with care,
The heart's warmest welcome would smile on me there;
No more from that doorstep again would I roam:
Be it ever so humble, there's no place like home.
  Home! Home! Sweet, sweet home!
  Be it ever so humble,
  There's no place like home.

See how—in spite of the absence of years—
How sweet the remembrance of home still appears.
From attractions abroad which but flatter the eye,
The unsatisfied heart turns, and says, with a sigh:
    Home! Home! Sweet, sweet home!
    There's no place like home—
    No—there's no place like home.

How sweet it would be to see father's fond smile,
And the cares of my mother to soothe and beguile.
Let others delight in new pleasure to roam,
But give me—Oh! give me, the pleasures of home!
    Home! Home! Sweet, sweet home!
    Just give me, oh, give me
    The pleasures of home.
                 John Howard Payne

FRIENDS AND ENEMIES

E WHO has a thousand friends
    Has not a friend to spare,
While he who has one enemy
    Will meet him everywhere

ATTRIBUTED TO *Ralph Waldo Emerson*

[112]

ᥱᲥ PRAYER ᲥᲥ

ORE **THINGS** are wrought by prayer
Than this world dreams of. Wherefore, let your voice
Rise like a fountain for me night and day.
For what are men better than sheep or goats
That nourish a blind life within the brain,
If, knowing God, they lift not hands of prayer
Both for themselves and those who call them friend?
For so the whole round earth is every way
Bound by gold chains about the feet of God.

Alfred Lord Tennyson

ᥱᲥ THE GOLDEN SIDE ᲥᲥ

HERE is many a rest in the road of life,
If we only would stop to take it;
And many a note from the better land,
If the querulous heart would wake it.
To the sunny soul that is full of hope
And whose true trust is never failing,
The grass is green and the flowers are bright,
Though the wintry storm's prevailing.

[113]

Better to hope, though the clouds hang low,
  And to keep your eyes up-lifted;
For the sweet blue sky will soon shine through
  When the ominous clouds are rifted.
There was never a night without a day,
  Or an evening without a morning;
And the darkest hour, as the proverb goes,
  Is the hour before the dawning.

There is many a gem in the path of life
  Which we pass in our idle pleasure,
That is richer far than the jewelled crown
  Or the miser's hoarded treasure;
It may be the love of a little child,
  Or a mother's prayer to Heaven,
Or only a beggar's grateful thanks
  For a cup of water given.

Better to weave in the web of life
  A bright and golden filling,
And to do God's will with a ready heart
  And hands that are swift and willing,
Than to snap the delicate, slender threads
  Of our curious lives asunder,
And then blame Heaven for the tangled ends,
  And sit and grieve and wonder.

Bertha W. Davidson

⊰ OPPORTUNITY ⊱

ASTER of human destinies am I!
Fame, love, and fortune on my footsteps wait.
Cities and fields I walk; I penetrate
Deserts and seas remote, and passing by
House, estate or office—soon or late
I knock unbidden once at every gate!

"If sleeping, wake—if eating, rise before
I turn away. It is the hour of fate,
And they who follow me reach every state
Mortals desire, and conquer every foe
Save death; but those who doubt or hesitate,
Condemned to failure, penury, and woe,
Seek me in vain and uselessly implore.

"I answer not, and I return no more!"

John James Ingalls

⊰ BED IN SUMMER ⊱

N WINTER I get up at night
And dress by yellow candle-light.
In summer quite the other way,
I have to go to bed by day.

I have to go to bed and see
 The birds still hopping on the tree,
Or hear the grown-up people's feet
 Still going past me in the street.

And does it not seem hard to you,
 When all the sky is clear and blue,
And I should like so much to play,
 I have to go to bed by day?

Robert Louis Stevenson

✌ CHARTLESS ☙

 NEVER saw a moor,
 I never saw the sea,
 Yet know I how the heather looks,
 And what a wave must be.

I never spoke with God,
 Nor visited in heaven;
Yet certain am I of the spot
 As if the chart were given.

Emily Dickinson

KNOW, as my life grows older,
    And my eyes have clearer sight,
    That under each rank wrong somewhere
      There lies the root of right;
That each sorrow has its purpose,
  By the sorrowing oft unguessed;
But as sure as the sun brings morning,
  Whatever is—is best.

I know that each sinful action,
  As sure as the night brings shade,
Is somewhere, sometime punished,
  Though the hour be long delayed.
I know that the soul is aided
  Sometimes by the heart's unrest,
And to grow means often to suffer—
  But whatever is—is best.

I know there are no errors,
  In the great eternal plan,
All things work together
  For the final good of man.
And I know when my soul speeds onward,
  In its grand eternal quest,
I shall say as I look back earthward,
  "Whatever is—is best."

Ella Wheeler Wilcox

❧ INDEX OF FIRST LINES ☙

[124]

John Scott, a native of Trenton, New Jersey, has for a quarter of a century been with Radio Station WOR, where he is currently a newscaster and the focal man of the magazine-type program "Radio New York." A graduate in journalism from Kent State University, Scott—after his Army service—joined WOR and announced, directed, or produced a number of local and network radio and television shows in the news and documentary field while covering news stories that ranged from riots to medical conventions and even took him overseas. Scott maintains an active role in religious and civic activities. He is married, the father of two children, and lives—as he works—in the heart of Manhattan.

This book was designed for Oak Tree Press
by Ernst Reichl. The type used is Granjon.
It was set by The Book Press Incorporated
in Brattleboro, Vermont.